Memories of the Past and Today

Sandy Smith

The names in the book have been changed. They are being anonymous to protect their identity. Their first names have been changed.

This book is based on a true story. There are chapters that aren't changed. Chapters that I thought about. A few chapters have a twist. Depends on how you look at it.

Contents

Memories of the Past

Growing up in a small town, everyone knows you by your face. People walking past, saying hi and how are you. As that person strikes up a conversation with you about lost times, you're like, "WOW." I didn't know that.

As the years went past, you lost all touch with that person. One day you get to thinking about that person, until one day you see the spouse, the kids, or someone who knew that person. Then you come to find out that the person that you were thinking about passed away.

You are at a loss for words and couldn't get the words that you want to say. You walked away, the news leaving you speechless and much more. Knowing that you couldn't get that person out of your head. As you think of the moments that you had with that person. You tend to laugh and or cry. Maybe you are puzzled. Trying to figure out what that memory meant.

When you got home, your spouse and children were waiting for you to get home. When you walked through the door looking sad and lost. Your spouse and children asked you what's wrong. When you told them the sad news. They were in shock. They didn't know what to think or what to say. They were speechless.

They young child left the room crying. The young child didn't understand what had happened to the elderly guy. The young child felt like she lost a family member.

The child's parent comes into her room and comforts the child. The parent explained to the young child that things like this tends to happen when we get older. The parent explained to the young child. The young child gave her parent a hug and said thank you for explaining it to me and making me understand. The parent picked her up and went to the front room.

One day that the couple and their children were out and seen the kids. Everyone was at a loss for words and they didn't know what to say. They went on with their business. Nothing was said till the elderly woman seen the young girl crying. The adult went over to the child and gave the child a hug. Knowing that the young child loved her husband.

After what happened, the elderly woman asked the child's parents. The parents promised to have their child to come over since they were neighbors, so the child's parents allowed for their girl to go next door and visit.

The elderly woman showed the child pictures of the spouse and home videos. The child became close to the elderly woman. During the summer, the child spent days with the elderly woman to keep her company. She found out days later that the elderly woman was related to the young girl, the young girl's siblings, and the child's dad.

The child recognized a picture and mentioned it to the elderly woman. That the picture is of her great-grandma. The elderly woman looked at the child speechless and didn't know what to say. The elderly woman didn't realize that the young girl's dad was her husband's great-nephew.

The young girl told her dad that the guy is his great-uncle and showed the picture of the young girl-s great-grandma to her dad. The dad was speechless. The young girl's dad called his mom and the mother came over to the great-aunt's house. They were all in shock. But they were happy. They became close. They were one big family.

Marie

Marie was born on a January day of 1975 to the parents of Maggie and Gene. Maggie wanted to name her baby girl Hazel Blanche. An family member said, the hell you are! So Maggie went with the name Marie Gale. Why? Gale is Maggie's middle name.

When Maggie and Gene brought their baby girl home, they were looking forward to settle in for the afternoon.

As they got settled in, their oldest daughter was looking forward to having an younger sibling and to have someone to play with. As the girls were growing up, they had their days.

As Maggie was getting ready to take the girls to Savannah, MO and or Saint Joseph, MO, Mrs. Logan came over to look after the girls. The oldest girl (June) decided to put baby powder in her baby sister's face. Ms. Logan checked in on the girls to see what was going on. Mrs. Logan rushed to Marie to clean her up and get the baby powder off Marie's face. Marie couldn't breathe. Good thing Mrs. Logan saved the day.

Marie was always a happy baby. When Marie was fussy, she would cry for her mom. One day, Maggie didn't hear Marie cry. Mag went into Marie's room and picked her up and gave her her bottle. Mag rocked her back to sleep after giving Marie her bottle. Mag is Marie's great-grandma and Maggie's grandma.

As Mag rocked her great-granddaughter back to sleep, that she sang a song that was so smoothly. Marie had her hand around her great grandma's thumb. Mag just loved her great-granddaughter.

When Marie was about the ages of 4 or 5 that she had a mole taken off from her face that sat between her eyes.

Marie had an speech problem. Marie went to this school to get help with her speech problem. Marie went to this school to get help with her speech delay. Marie started to talk better. Her words made sense.

The school teachers helped her to talk better. Marie really liked her teachers. Connie Evans is one she really liked. Marie can't think of the black guy's name from the school she went to but she liked him too. Marie thinks of that school from time to time.

When Marie was about the ages of 6 or 7 years old, her sister June dared her to climb up on this green metal electric box. (These metal electric boxes were two sizes and had these rubber type thing on the side of the box.) Marie cut her leg. Marie was rushed to the Med Clinic there in Savannah, MO.

Dr. Baker had to put stitches in Marie's leg. As Marie was laying on the bed, she was held down. Marie used words that wasn't nice at the doctor and the ones who were holding her down. When it was done, Marie felt bad about what she had done. The thing is that Marie didn't blame the doctor, the nurses, and everybody who was holding her down. Marie blamed her sister for what had happened to her leg.

As Marie's parents are divorced, she tends to stay to herself. When Marie was 14 ½ years old, she was placed in a foster home. Her mom had tapes that shouldn't have been seen. They were porn. The guy (Kim) turned her in to the DFS. When Maggie seen the people come to her door, she wasn't happy. Maggie felt bad and ashamed. She thought to herself. Why did I have them porn in my room? Maggie felt like a bad mom.

Marie thought that her mom felt like she's a bad mom. When Marie was in the second foster home, she really loved her foster mom, foster sister, and foster brother.

When Marie moved to Saint Joseph, MO in 1997, she had worked at a place for special needs people. Marie didn't feel like she fitted in with the others so she quit.

In March of 1998, Marie met a guy who was 11 years older than her. When Marie meet David, she felt like she met her match.

In their first year of their relationship, David taught her the things that Marie needed to learn. Now as Marie is in her 40's, Marie doesn't allow people (such as her family and friends) to walk all over her and much more. Marie had grown up a lot over the last 19 years. Marie is thankful that David taught her how to stand up for herself.

David had taught Marie on how to cook and bake. Then Marie started to be a better cook. Marie started to come up with her own recipes. David's mom had loved her (Marie's) cooking. Today Marie is thankful to have David and his family in her life.

Maggie

Maggie thought to herself, when she was old enough that she would learn how to cook and bake. Maggie's mom Blanche taught her about what she knows. When Maggie left home, she got married and had two girls. Maggie thought she was a good wife and mother until she felt like she failed.

As Maggie was married and had her girls under one roof, Maggie would coupon to a save money. She would help her husband (Maggie's daughter's dad) to pick up cans and anything Maggie could do to bring in extra money, knowing that she was on SSI.

Over the years that Maggie met people, these people didn't see the disability that Maggie had. These people come to like Maggie for who she was.

When Maggie's dad passed away on Christmas Day of 1960, she was 8 years old. As Maggie got older and had her two girls, she never cared for Christmas. When Marie asked her mom why she didn't like Christmas, Maggie told her that her dad passed on that day. On Christmas Day, all Maggie had were memories of her dad. Maggie didn't talk about her dad to June and Marie. Maggie talked about her mom Blanche.

Gene

Gene had worked most of his life working at the sale barn, to working on the farm, to working at a grocery store, to working at a car wash. Gene would pick up cans when he can. When Gene and Maggie divorced he never stopped loving his girls. Gene had missed so much in his daughters' lives. At least that Marie kept in touch by letters.

Gene knew that Maggie couldn't keep his girls away from him like she wished. Knowing that Maggie tried her best.

Gene knew what he had done to his oldest daughter was wrong. The story behind it was that Maggie set him up to it. The story was wrong. The family didn't want to believe what Marie saw. Knowing that Marie witnessed what had happened.

The doctor said that she (June) had been touched. Marie's families blamed her for what had happened. Years later, that the families felt bad on making Marie a liar. The families blamed her (Marie) for breaking Marie's family up. They don't know how to apologize to Marie or June. They just let it go.

Gene thought to himself when his girls got older that Gene would tell June and Marie the truth on what had happened. Gene apologized for what he had done and wanted his girls to forgive him. June and Marie had forgave their dad on what had happened. Gene was thrilled to have his girls forgive him. Gene never wanted to lose contact with his girls ever again.

Gene passed away on Father's Day of 2011. Gene took his feelings him to his grave. When Gene passed away that Marie wrote a poem for her dad. Only ones who read the poem is only Gene's girlfriend, Mari and God. The poem was heart-felt for Marie.

> Not ready to let you go
> I know that I hadn't been around as much,
> Knowing that it's hard to see you, Dad, at least
> that you know I love you with all my heart.
> You'll always have that place in my heart no

matter what.
I got to say though father
Just that I'm not ready to let you go father, It's
hard to say good bye to you so soon.
Please stay around a lot longer.
I'm not ready to let you go as of yet.

There's so much that I want to say that I never had
told you before, Father, as I thought of you often. It's
hard not to think of you and to tell you how much I
love you and how much I missed in your life.

June

June was born on a December day of 1971 to Maggie and Gene. Maggie and Gene were thrilled to be parents for the first time. Gene thought of the name Lynda, but decided to pass and went with June Louise.

June was their pride and joy. June's parents had thought about more kids. Maggie and Gene waited till they seen were they were with June. They wanted to be good parents.

As June was the only child, she felt like she was left out. June felt like she had no kids to play with. June loved the attention from her parents. She knew her parents loved her. June want a sibling to play with and she got her wish.

When June was growing up, that June was so wild that

her parents didn't know what to do with her. Maggie and Gene didn't want June to be wild and crazy. June was wild and June's parents couldn't control her, not whatsoever.

When June got out on her own, she finally settled down and had kids of her own. June's first marriage didn't turn out well. The guy that June was married to was 30 to 35 years older than her. June wanted to get away from her parents and left Marie alone. June wasn't always a happy go-getter like Marie was.

June loved her baby sister though. The thing is through that June and Marie had their fights. What sisters doesn't fight with each other? June knew that Marie looked up to her as a big sister.

Maggie, June, and Marie

There are a lot of broken homes. June and Marie had each other. June made sure that Marie was taken care of. Maggie tended to go out on the weekends as long as she had the money to go out to drink. Knowing that Maggie wasn't married and tied down. The only way for Maggie to unstress is to get out and meet people.

Maggie didn't know how to take care of her girls. Maggie was struggling to keep her girls fed and clothed. Maggie would go to the food pantry to get food to feed her girls.

June and Marie were taken away from Maggie. The girls were in foster homes. Even through June were in more foster homes than Marie. June was in 16 to 17 foster homes. June was hard to handle. Marie was in 2 foster homes. Marie was easy to get along with and got along with others.

June and Marie will never forget their memories of their parents. Now they are older and wiser. June and Marie are happier now. They try their best to not think about the past.

Maggie and Gene passed. They never stopped caring and loving their girls. They tried to be good parents.

Frank and Ilene

Frank loved his wife, Ilene. They had their ups and downs. Knowing that Frank and Ilene would do anything for each other. Frank and Ilene loved the farm life. They have five kids of their own. They raised their kids good and taught them how to treat others and much more. Four out of the five kids of Frank and Ilene moved out and started their own lives and their own families. They gave their parents grandchildren. Frank and Ilene were thrilled to be grandparents.

As their nine grandchildren were growing up, they brought joy to Frank and Ilene. Their grandchildren have their own stories about their grandparents farm. All nine grandchildren loved their grandparents.

Marie one of the nine grandchildren. When Marie was

about the ages of 6 through 8 years old her grandma called Marie, June, and their seven cousins to go in and eat. Marie, June, and their cousins were playing in their grandparents build that did have a door. All eight kids ran to the house.

Marie was the last one to leave. When Marie look down she saw a snake. Marie didn't move. She waited until the snake was gone. Marie ran to the house. Ilene asked Marie what kept her. Marie told her grandma on what had happened. Marie's grandma said that there are snakes there from time to time but not always.

Frank and Ilene cared, loved, and respected their kids and grandchildren.

When Ilene was at Swanson's, she was trying to remember on how to spell Swanson's. Ilene called her husband to come back over to write out the check. That's when Frank and their kids knew that she started to have Alzheimer's.

When Ilene passed away, her kids and grandchildren along with Frank took it hard. Marie overheard her grandpa saying to his girls. as his son and Marie were behind them. that it should have been me, not mom.

Marie was crushed to hear her grandpa say that. It was

hard for Marie to control her feelings. Marie wanted to cry when she heard her grandpa say that. Marie really loves her grandparents. Frank and Ilene were the only grandparents that she knew. Marie didn't know her Mom's (Maggie) parents. Maggie's dad past away December 25, 1960 and Maggie's mom past away September 6, 1971.

Frank and Ilene loved spending time with their family. Ilene was an amazing cook. Marie wanted to be like her grandma. Marie had thought about her grandma's meals and always wondered about her grandma's recipes.

Rest in Peace Grandpa and Grandma. You are missed by family and friends. We miss you both.

Home in Savannah, MO

As Gene and Maggie went to look at this house in Savannah, they knew it was the one. They were making payments for it. They wanted to raise their girls in this house. Gene, Maggie, June, and Marie had their moments. When Gene and Maggie divorced, Maggie, June, and Marie lived in this house for 4 to 6 years till Maggie couldn't afford the house.

This family has too many memories in this house. It tends to haunt June and Marie. They have their good and bad memories in this house. June and Marie blamed their mom for what their dad done to June at a young age. Gene, June, and Marie try not to let that memory get to them. They want to remember the good times. Knowing that Gene, Maggie, June, and Marie put those memories behind them and moved on with their own lives.

Family

Over the years, Marie always wondered about her family. Marie doesn't know nothing about her parents family. Marie wonders where her heritage is from, not knowing where Marie's family is from. They could be from Germany or wherever. Marie wishes she knew more about her family.

As long that her relatives knows (that knows Marie, June, Maggie, and Gene), Marie hopes that you'll find her. Marie wants to get to know you and know more about her family. Marie doesn't know a lot of her family. Knowing that Marie is surprised to meet her family that she never knew.

Between 2003 through 2008, Gene had mentioned to his girls (June and Marie) that he has another child. As

Marie has wondered to herself about this other child (not knowing if she has a half-sister and or a half-brother) of her dad's somewhere, Marie doesn't know how to go about finding this person that Gene told her girls about. As Marie asked herself these questions. Would Gene's sister know about this third child of their brother Gene's? Marie really wants to get to know these questions and to know her family.

All Marie wants to do is find her family and get to know them. Marie also wants to know Maggie's family. Knowing that Marie doesn't know a whole lot about her mom's family.

Dr. Baker

You were the best doctor that anyone could ask for.
You had delivered a lot of babies in your life time.
Knowing that I am one who was delivered by you.
You were amazing on what you've had done.

The Med Clinic misses you,
Your patients miss you
Your family misses you,
And you friends miss you.

You are still the talk of the town,
The babies you had delivered talks about you,
Your family and friends talk about you,
No matter where I am at that time - Your name is still
mentioned to this day.

As we tend to talk about you,
That we tend to carry you in our thoughts, prayers,

and in our memories,
You aren't far away when you are mentioned.
I want to say thank you for delivering me.

Melissa L. McCallon

Melissa had met a lot of people in her life. Friends came in and out of her life. Melissa had touched a lot of people in her lifetime.

June and Marie became best friends. They had their own little group of friends. Marie had thought of Melissa as a sister. Melissa was there when Marie needed someone to talk to. Marie didn't have a lot of friends to talk to and to understand what Marie was going through. Melissa had Marie's back. When June, Marie, Melissa, and their friends went on with their own lives, they lost contact with each other.

One day Marie was reading the St. Joseph News-Press and it caught her eyes. Marie couldn't believe what she was reading. Article read *Fire Kills 2 in Savannah*

Trailer. Marie's heart sank.

Marie was at a loss. She went off the deep end. Marie thought herself on why would a person take gasoline and a match and throw that match on the flame. Knowing that Melissa was a mom to a beautiful baby girl.

Melissa's daughters lost both of their parents. The baby didn't know her parents. All she has is pictures of her parents and the story that her family and friends told her about her parents.

Melissa, you are thought of by your family and friends. We all miss you so much.

There were days that Marie had thought about Melissa. Marie thought to herself how Melissa is and how she turned out in her life. Marie asks herself on why a person had to take Melissa away from her own daughter.

Even though that Marie had never meet Melissa's daughter, Marie had thought about Melissa's daughter is reading this chapter. Marie wants you to know that Marie has thought about your mom. Marie really misses your mom a lot. Your mom had touched Marie's life in so many ways that Marie doesn't know how to explain it. Marie thought of your mom as a sister and her very best friend. You are blessed to have her as your mom. Knowing that you had never known her. Your mom was the most caring, loving and sweetest person that Marie had ever known.

Rest in Peace Melissa,

You are missed.

David and Marie

They met at a bar in March of 1998. Marie was watching David. David caught Marie looking at him. When David was through playing pool, he came over to talk to a guy and Maggie dared Marie to go to David. Marie was scared at first but Marie went over to David.

When David got done talking to the guy, Marie asked him to dance. Knowing that a guy asks the girl to dance instead of the girl asking the guy to dance. David and Marie danced to a slow song. When the song was over, Marie and David went outside and talked for 30 to 45 minutes. They hit it off. David and Marie became a couple.

Marie told David about her past. After David and Marie moved in together, David taught Marie the things that she needed to know. Marie finally stood up for herself to people. Today Marie doesn't let people walk all over her. Marie had once let her mom and her sister walk all over her. Not today. Marie found peace in herself and finding herself.

To David and to the Cline family. Marie is thankful to have you in her life. Marie didn't know what family felt like until she's been around you. Knowing that Marie missed it on being around her own family. Marie wasn't around her family growing up after her parents divorced. Marie felt alone and left out of her family's life. You as the Cline family had filled that empty spot in Marie's life.

After years of not having someone to love, care, respect, taught Marie and much more that Marie would been the same person as she was. Marie really came a long way in her life with you David and the Cline family. Thank you for everything you shown to Marie. Marie is thankful to have someone to love and much more.

Marie thinks of David and the Cline family as her family. David and family, thank you for being a part of Marie's life and teaching Marie what she needs to know. Marie loves you all so much.

Homeless People

There are a lot of people in this world that are homeless. They are living on the streets and wherever they can find a place to sleep. These homeless people had either got kicked out of their spouse or family member's place. They could've been homeless by being kicked (thrown out) of their rental place. They may have a drug problem or a drinking problem or both. They could have their home caught on fire. It all depends on what had happened to that person or persons with their family members.

There are homeless people who don't want you to feel sorry for them. They feel bad the way it is. All they want is to get their lives straightened out and they don't know how. These homeless people tend to do what they can to get back on their own. They want to do it on their own. Them homeless people want to do thing the way they know. As long as that they need help, they'll always ask for the help they need.

These homeless people never know where they are going to land. All they have is their spirits. Those homeless people never know what will come their way.

St. Joseph Transit

When Marie moved to Saint Joseph, Marie asked her mom how she was going to get around, because Saint Joseph is a lot bigger than Savannah. Maggie and Marie had walked everywhere in Savannah. Maggie said to Marie, I am going to teach you the ropes. Marie asked her mom what she meant. Maggie said, "Let's go."

Maggie and Marie walked down the hill of North 11th. Maggie took her daughter Marie to this stop for the bus depot sign. As they waited for the bus to get there, Maggie said, "Look, that's the bus that will take you where you need to go." Maggie showed Marie where to go to the bus depot to get on the next bus to go to wherever Marie needed to go.

After Marie got the hang of it, she knows where she's

going. If Marie doesn't know where the place is at, she'll ask the driver and the driver will let her know. Even though that Marie doesn't take the bus, she'll walk where she knows where she can walk to. Marie tends to check her surrounding as Marie walks to these places.

There were a lot of bus drivers that came and went. Marie had met a lot of nice drivers. Marie knew one from Savannah. There was one gal that Marie didn't realize was Mrs. Down's sister until months later. Jane tends to crack Marie up.

Once a person gets to know the routes, they'll get used to riding the bus and know it. The drivers are helpful. The drivers can be your friends.

To the Saint Joseph Transit. Marie wants to say thank you for all your help on getting her where she needed to go. Marie will have a special place for you in her heart.

Thank you.

Hair Donations

When Marie was told by Mrs. Hart about Locks of Love, Marie thought that she would donate her hair instead of the salon trashing her hair. Knowing that Marie's hair grows so fast. The thing is though, there are people who likes/loves Marie's long hair on her. Sometimes it's an hassle for Marie to deal with her hair. When Marie tends to have her hair cut, she never wants her hair to be short short. Maggie tended to have her hair short like a man. Not Marie. Knowing that Marie doesn't tend to have it short.

There are a lot of people today that hair tends to grow so fast on a person. Knowing that a person doesn't donate their hair. It's that person's choice on what he or she wants to do with their hair. There are places that you can donate your hair to. They are Locks of

Love, Wigs for Kids, and Pantene. Those are a few that Marie had heard of that takes your hair to make wigs.

There's a site that Marie searched on Google. It's called HairSellon. Looking at the site that a person would buy your hair. That you pick your price on how much you want to sell our hair for. It's your choice on what you want to do with your hair.

Made in the USA
Columbia, SC
17 July 2018